Terry Shade & Jeremy Woolstenhulme

STRING BASICS™
STEPS TO SUCCESS FOR STRING ORCHESTRA

Welcome to **String Basics Book 3**. We are proud that you have entered a new and exciting year in your orchestra program. You will find that **Book 3** has many similarities to **String Basics Books 1** and **2** because it includes a strong mixture of technical studies (left hand and bow arm), as well as a nice selection of classical tunes and melodies representing different cultures from around the world. A variety of duets, chorales, and orchestra arrangements are included to round out the book. Music theory and composition exercises are featured to help you become a well-rounded musician.

As you continue on your journey to becoming a more advanced player, **Book 3** will help you broaden your knowledge of your instrument in many ways; tuning your own instrument, shifting, learning advanced time signatures and key signatures, playing more difficult rhythms, harmonics, trills, and grace notes. You will also begin the initial steps toward learning vibrato!

If you have been practicing with a metronome up to this point, congratulations! Continue working with your metronome throughout **Book 3** as it will be beneficial. If you are new to working with a metronome, now is the perfect time to include it into your daily practice routine. Using a metronome is one of many steps to take toward becoming a strong and successful musician.

Best wishes,

Terry Shade

Jeremy Woolstenhulme

ISBN-10: 0-8497-3517-3 • ISBN-13: 978-0-8497-3517-2

©2013 Kjos Music Press, Neil A. Kjos Music Company, Distributor, 4382 Jutland Drive, San Diego, California, 92117.
International copyright secured. All rights reserved. Printed in U.S.A.

Tuning Your Bass

Before beginning the tuning process, take a look at the pegs & peg box, the tailpiece, and the bridge. In the photos here, notice how the strings cleanly wrap around the pegs. Examine which strings wraps around which peg. The tuning pegs on a bass are called Machine Pegs or Geared Pegs. These pegs have a gear mechanism that is especially designed for turning thick strings on the peg and adjusting the tension on the string.

If you look at the tailpiece you will notice that there are no fine tuners like the other string instruments in the orchestra because the machine pegs allow for fine tuning and the tuners on the tailpiece are not necessary.

Finally, take a close look at the strings where they nestle into the grooves on the crown (top of the bridge).

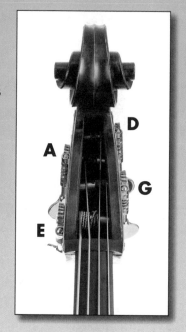

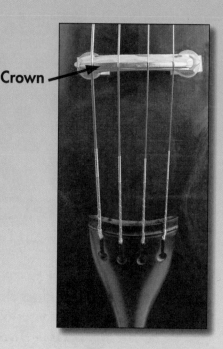

Crown

To begin, have a reference pitch that can sustain a continuous tone. Start with A-440. Listen to the A pitch and ask yourself: Is my A higher or lower, or in tune (identical) to the given A? You may also want to use a needle or dial tuner. These tuners indicate when the string is flat or sharp depending on what the needle is telling you. If the needle is lined up with the note, then the string is in tune. Make sure the tuner is calibrated to 440, unless directed otherwise.

Tuning With Machine Pegs (Arco) – G String Demonstration

• Place your bow on the G string and play it softly (so that you can also hear the reference pitch).

• Reach your left hand up and make sure that you are touching the G tuning peg.

• Pinch the metal peg between your thumb and your rounded index finger.

• Turn the gear peg clockwise to raise the pitch of your string or turn it counterclockwise to lower the pitch.

• Work toward matching the two pitches perfectly. It may be necessary to tilt your head closer to the bass neck to better hear yourself.

• Begin tuning the bass strings in this order: start with A, then D, G, and finally down to low E.

Video Lesson #4

Tuning With Harmonics

The open string on a string bass can be very low and difficult to hear when tuning your bass in an orchestra. One option to better hear the pitch of the string is to use harmonics for tuning. Harmonics are played by bowing the string and lightly touching the finger on a natural harmonic point on the string. See page 24 for more information about playing harmonics or view the video lesson, **Harmonics.**

You can play an octave higher on the string by lightly placing only the 3rd finger down on the string at the mid point between the nut and the bridge. By dividing the string in half you get the octave sound from the open string. Playing the octaves on the string can help you to hear the sound more clearly and make an accurate match with the tuning pitch.

- There are more harmonics found on the bass string than just the mid-point octave.
- While playing the A string, you can find the second octave A by dividing the string into 4 parts and placing your 1st finger on the A string where you would normally play the note D.
- Only touch the first finger to the string without fully pressing the string down. This harmonic A will sound 2 octaves higher than the open string A.
- In that same position, lightly place your 4th finger down on the D String where you would normally play the note A. If you remove the finger pressure and only touch the 4th finger lightly to the string you will get the same harmonic A you were just playing on the A string.
- Compare this harmonic A with the one that is found on the A string. They should sound the same if the strings are in tune.

Tuning Process with Harmonics

- Make sure the A string is in tune before comparing the harmonics of the other strings.
- Compare the Harmonic A on the A string with the harmonic A found on the D string at the end of the neck. If they sound the same that means your D string is in tune.
- Now with the 1st finger on the D string, place this where you would normally play the note G. Lightly touch the 1st finger to the string and you will get harmonic D, two octaves above the open D string. To find harmonic D on the G string place your 4th finger where you normally play D and release the pressure. Compare these harmonic D's found on both the strings. If the two harmonic D's sound the same that means your G string is in tune.
- Lastly, follow the same procedure to check and see if the E string is in tune. Stay in the same position and place your 1st finger on the E string where you would normally play the note A, this is harmonic E. Compare the harmonic sound with that found on the A string using harmonic 4th finger where you would normally play the note E. If they sound the same that means your E string is in tune. If not then adjust the E string until it matches the E harmonic found on the A string.

Successful Tuning Tips

1. Ask your teacher for help if your tuning pegs are difficult to turn.

2. If your instrument is severely out of tune to begin with, you will probably need to retune it several times.

3. If a string has become loose, be sure that the string is sitting in the groove on the crown of the bridge before tightening it with the gear peg.

4. When tuning your strings in orchestra class, play softly.

5. Learning to tune your own instrument is an ongoing process and it takes practice, patience, and some skills. Quite simply, the more you do it, the easier it becomes!

Steps to Success:
- ❏ Establish group pulse
- ❏ Play with good intonation and tone

1. D Major

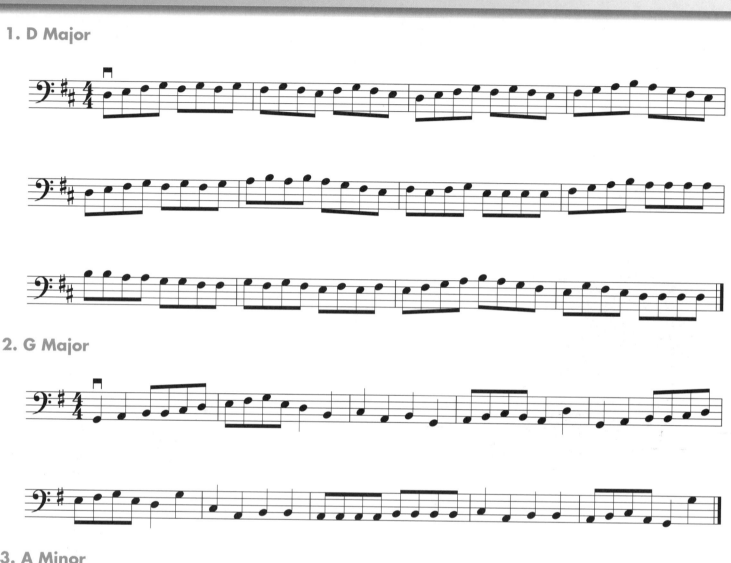

2. G Major

3. A Minor

4. D Minor

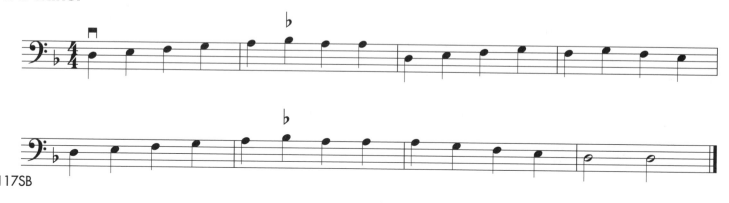

Review: Bowing Exercises — String Crossings

Steps to Success:
- ❏ Hold bow correctly
- ❏ Play using three different bow arm levels

A string level

D string level

G string level

5. Open String Slurs

6. Separate Crossings

7. Careful Bowings

8. Three String Slur

9. The Swift Up Bow

10. All About the Bow

rit.

Review: Finger Patterns

Steps to Success:
- ❑ Play D Major 1-4 finger pattern
- ❑ Play D Minor 1-2 finger pattern
- ❑ Play G Minor with low 1st finger on B♭

1-4 finger pattern

1-2 finger pattern

low 1st finger on B♭, 4th finger on C

11. D to A in D Major

12. Musette

Johann Sebastian Bach (1685–1750)
German Composer

Allegro

f

13. D to A in D Minor

14. Minuet   **TEST LINE**

Johann Sebastian Bach (1685–1750)
German Composer

Moderato

mf

15. Pat-A-Pan

French Carol

Allegro

½ Pos.   *mf*

f

p

Review: Low 1st Finger

Steps to Success:
- ❏ Identify half steps and whole steps
- ❏ Play ½ position
- ❏ Understand and play *a tempo*
- ❏ Identify major and minor key signatures

a tempo = return to the original tempo after a *ritard.* or a fermata

16. Open Pattern

17. Challenger Deep

Moderato

½ Pos. *mf*

18. B♭ to E♭ in B♭ Major

Andante

19. The Rakes of Mallow

Irish Folk Song

Allegro

mf

a tempo

rit. *f*

20. Steps to Learning Theory

Name the major key for each key signature below.

_____   _____   _____   _____

8

Review: High 3rd Finger (Violin, Viola)/Forward Extension (Cello)

Steps to Success:
- ❏ Shift to C♯ and D on the G string
- ❏ Play staccato

4th finger on D

21. The C♯ Stretch – *Duet*

22. Now Is the Month of Maying

Thomas Morley (1559–1602)
English Composer

23. Theme from "Serenade for Strings"

Peter Ilyich Tchaikovsky (1840–1893)
Russian Composer

24. Coventry Carol

English Carol

Steps to Success:

❏ Identify and play Louré bowing

❏ Understand **Adagio**

> Louré = long hooked legato notes with the bow. There is slight separation between the slurred notes.

> Adagio = slow tempo, slower than **Andante**

25. Louré – *Quartet*

26. Las Mañanitas

Mexican Folk Song

27. Danny Boy

Irish Folk Song

Steps to Success:
- ❏ Place 1st finger on G#
- ❏ Understand A Major key signature
- ❏ Play A Major Scale

E A D G

G#

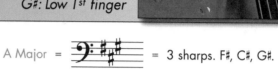

G#: Low 1st finger

A Major = 🎼 = 3 sharps. F#, C#, G#.

28. Going for G# – *Duet*

A

½ Pos.

B

29. Let's Take Turns

Andante

Everyone   Cello/Bass   Viola   Violin

30. A Major Scale – *Memorization Line*

31. Sicilian Hymn

Traditional

Moderato

mf

mp   *mf*

f

32. Bella Bimba

Italian Folk Song

Allegro

mf

A Major/E String Note: G# (Violin, Bass)

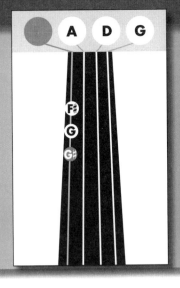

Steps to Success:
- Place 4th finger on G#

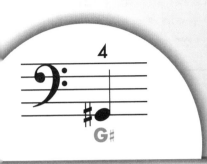

4th finger on G#

33. G# on E String – *New Step for Violin and Bass*

34. Upper Octave A Major Scale – *New Step for Violin*

35. Chester

William Billings (1746–1800)
American Composer

TEST LINE

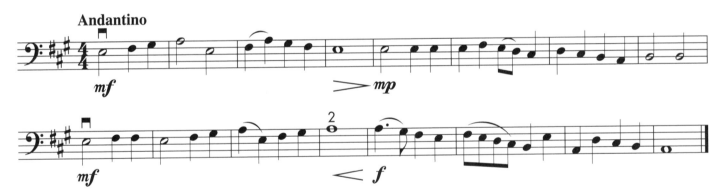

36. Gentle Mother

Japanese Folk Song

37. Minuet

Alexander Reinagle (1756–1809)
American Composer

Steps to Success:

❏ Play sixteenth notes

❏ Play eighth & sixteenth note combinations

❏ Play near the bridge and use less bow

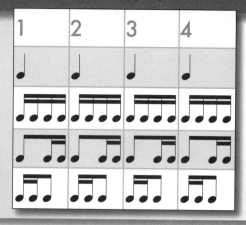

38. Sixteenth and Eighth Notes Reunion – *Trio*

Use less bow and play close to the bridge.

39. Rhythmic Scale in G Major – *Steps to Learning Theory*

Write in the counts before playing.

40. Sourwood Mountain

American Folk Song

41. Cripple Creek

American Folk Song

42. B♭ Major Scale in 92 Notes!

½ Pos.

43. Tirra Lirra Loo

Canadian Folk Song

Moderato

Fine

D.C. al Fine

f   *p*   *mf*

44. A Major Broken Thirds and Arpeggio

45. When I Was a Lad from "H.M.S. Pinafore"

Sir Arthur Sullivan (1843–1900)
English Composer

Allegro

f

46. Steps to Learning Theory 👣

Complete each measure using these notes: ♫♫ ♫♩ ♩♫. Check the time signature. Write in the counting and perform your new rhythm line on open D.

Steps to Success:
❏ Understand **Andantino**

Andantino = a tempo slightly faster than **Andante** and slower than **Moderato**

sim. = *simile* = continue playing in the same way

47. Dance – *Duet*

Daniel Gottlob Türk (1750–1813)
German Composer

48. Theme from "William Tell Overture" – *Orchestra Arrangement*

Gioacchino Rossini (1792–1868)
Italian Composer

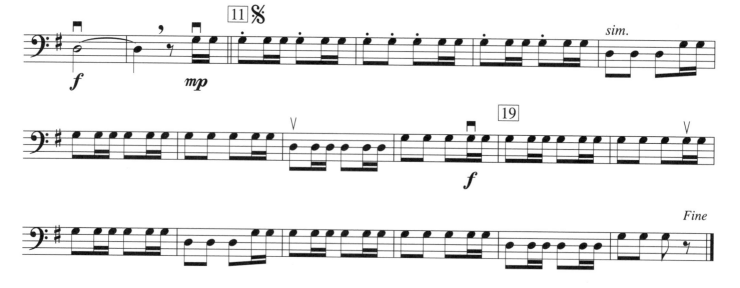

Dotted Eighth & Sixteenth Note Combinations

Steps to Success:
- ❏ Count and play dotted eighth & sixteenth note combinations
- ❏ Play dotted rhythms using hooked bowings
- ❏ Play dotted rhythms using slurs
- ❏ Understand *D.S. al Coda*

Dotted Eighth & Sixteenth Note Combination = ♪. ♬ = 1 beat

D.S. al Coda (Dal Segno al Coda) = go back to the sign 𝄋 and play until reaching "*To Coda* ⊕," then jump to the Coda.

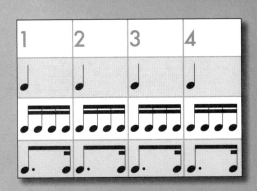

49. Dotted Eighth & Sixteenth Drill – *Duet*

50. Barnyard – *Duet*

51. Battle Cry of Freedom

George F. Root (1825–1895)
American Composer

52. The Golden Hook

53. Bridal Chorus from "Lohengrin"

Richard Wagner (1813–1883)
German Composer

54. Battle Hymn of the Republic

American Civil War Hymn

55. Hey, Ho, Nobody Home – *Round*

TEST LINE

English Carol

56. Theme from Symphony No. 8 "Unfinished"

Franz Schubert (1797–1828)
Austrian Composer

Chromatic Scale

Steps to Success:
- ❏ Understand and play chromatic melodies
- ❏ Play C chromatic scale

> Chromatic Scale = a series of 12 ascending or descending half steps

57. Chromatic Scale Prep

58. Chromatic Study

59. C Chromatic Scale

60. Habanera

Georges Bizet (1838–1875)
French Composer

61. La Cumparsita – *Orchestra Arrangement*

Gerardo H. Matos Rodríguez (1897–1948)
Uruguayan Composer

Steps to Success:

❏ Execute correct sliding motion of shifting to note G
❏ Play with proper left hand shape
❏ Identify hand placements according to given fingerings

Shift to G: Slide 1st finger on the D string towards the bridge. The hand, including the thumb, moves as a unit.

62. Shifting to 3rd Position – *Duet*

63. Totally in 3rd Position

64. Sliding to G with First Finger

65. Sliding to D with First Finger

Steps to Success:

❑ Play and understand shifting on the D and G strings

❑ Play 4th finger E on the G string

1st finger on D, 4th finger on E

66. Heading Up on D and A Strings

D Str.

67. Cellists Go to the 4th

68. Reaching for the Stars

69. Autumn from "The Four Seasons"

Antonio Vivaldi (1678–1741)
Italian Composer

Allegro

mf   *f*   *rit.*

70. G Major Scale in Position – *Memorization line*

Steps to Success:

❑ Execute correct sliding motion of shifting (up and back) with left hand

❑ Identify left hand position according to given fingerings

71. Sliding Between 1ˢᵗ & 3ʳᵈ Positions

72. Sliding Along

73. The Sugar Glider – *Duet*

74. Fleeting Years

Stephen Foster (1826–1864)
American Composer

75. Oh! Susanna

Extended 3rd Position (Cello)/Shifting Higher (Bass)

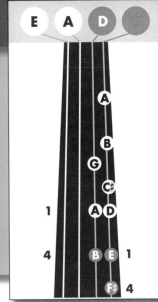

Steps to Success:
- ❏ Understand modulation
- ❏ Play high E and F♯ on the G string

> Modulation = changing from one key to another

1st finger on E, 4th finger on F♯

76. Extended 3rd Position for Cello

D Str.

77. At Pierrot's Door – *Duet – New Step for Bass*

French Folk Song

78. Ye Banks and Braes o' Bonnie Doon

Scottish Folk Song

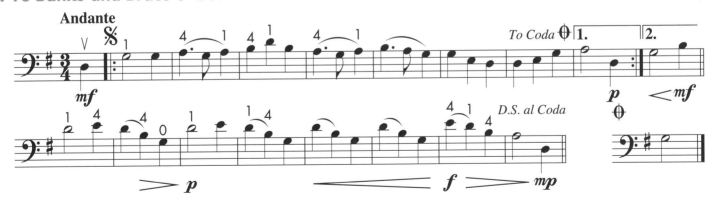

79. Mo Li Hua [Beautiful Jasmine Flower]

Chinese Folk Song

Steps to Success:
- ❏ Understand and play correct fingerings for given intervals
- ❏ Play on correct string according to given fingerings
- ❏ Play in position with good tone and accurate rhythm

80. Rainbow Vista

81. Petroglyphs

82. Waltz of the White Domes

83. The Old Brass Wagon – *Duet*

American Folk Song

84. The Technician's Overhaul

85. The Roly Poly Water Drops – *Duet*

86. Camptown Races

Stephen Foster (1826–1864)
American Composer

87. March from "Scipio" TEST LINE

George Frideric Handel (1685–1759)
English Composer

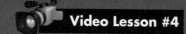

Steps to Success:

❏ Play harmonics on each string with proper technique and posture

❏ Play glissando up to natural harmonic

Glissando = gliding or sliding from one note to another

Natural Harmonic = special flute-like tones created by lightly touching the string at the mid-point

harmonics hand posture

88. Harmonics

Lightly touch the string with the 3rd finger.

89. Going the Octave with Harmonics

90. Glissando Road

91. Shifting to Harmonics

92. Harmonic Waltz – *Duet*

Steps to Success:
❑ Play harmonic G on G String

93. Up to Harmonic G

94. G Major Scale

95. Up to the Stratosphere – *New Step for Violin*

96. D Major Scale – *New Step for Violin – Duet*

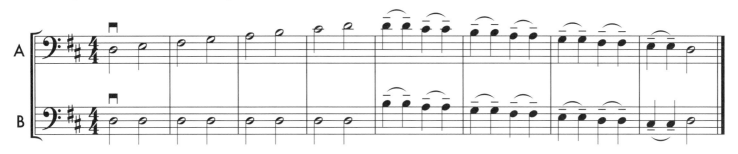

97. John Peel

English Folk Song

Shape Shifter

for String Orchestra

Jeremy Woolstenhulme (b.1974)
American Composer

117SB

Steps to Success:

❏ Count and play eighth note triplets
❏ Identify and play bow retrievals

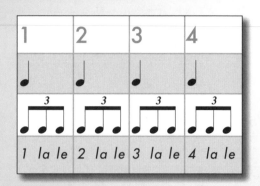

98. Playing Triplets

Name the scale featured in this exercise. _____

99. Three in One

100. Triplet Scale – *Memorization line*

101. Theme from "Zampa"

Ferdinand Hérold (1791–1833)
French Composer

102. Triumphal March from "Aida"

Giuseppe Verdi (1813–1901)
Italian Composer

Slow $\frac{6}{8}$ Time (Counting in 6)

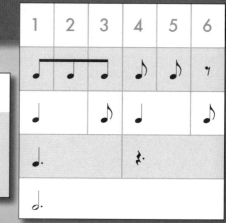

Steps to Success:

- ❏ Play and count $\frac{6}{8}$ time (slow tempo)
- ❏ Conduct slow tempo $\frac{6}{8}$ pattern

Time Signature (Slow) = $\frac{6}{8}$ = beats per measure
= ♪ receives 1 beat

Conducting Pattern = = A 6-beat pattern

103. Slow $\frac{6}{8}$

104. Scale in $\frac{6}{8}$

105. Quarters & Eighths

106. Romanza from Sonatina

Ludwig van Beethoven (1770–1827)
German Composer

107. Sumer Is Icumen In – *Steps to Learning Theory*

13th Century English Folk Song

Draw in the barlines, then play.

1	la	le	2	la	le

Steps to Success:
- ❑ Play and count ⁶⁄₈ time (fast tempo)
- ❑ Play slurs and hooked bowings in ⁶⁄₈ time
- ❑ Play and understand **Presto**

Presto = very fast, faster than **Allegro**

Time Signature (Fast) = ⁶⁄₈ 6 = 2 beats per measure 8 = ♩. receives 1 beat

Conducting Pattern = = A 2-beat pattern

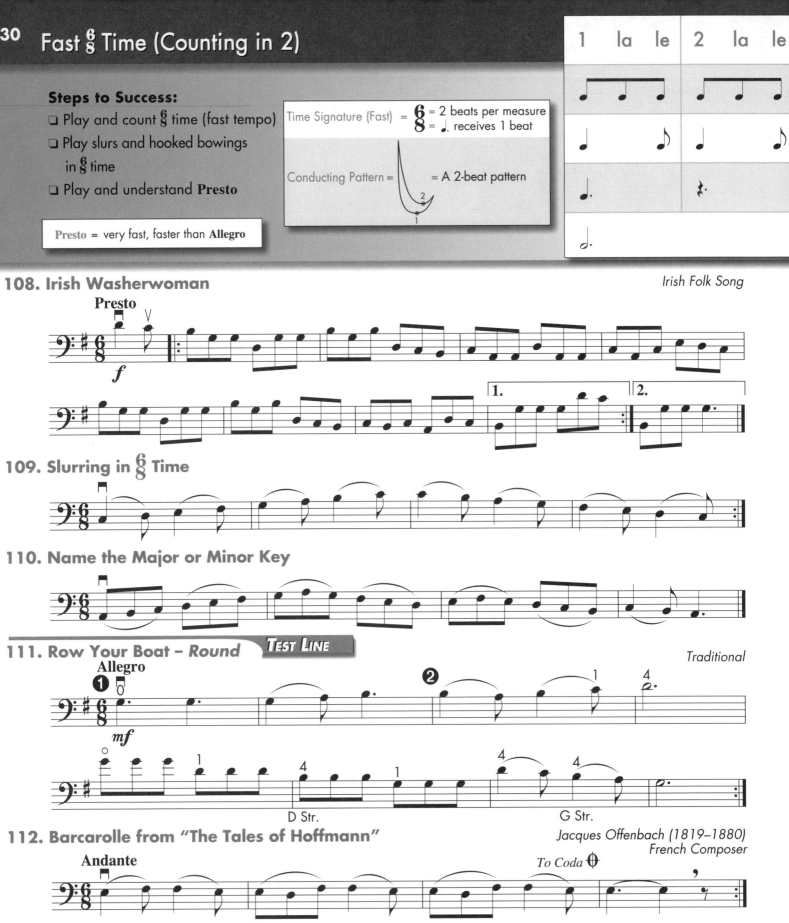

108. Irish Washerwoman
Irish Folk Song

Presto

𝆑

1.   2.

109. Slurring in ⁶⁄₈ Time

110. Name the Major or Minor Key

111. Row Your Boat – Round   TEST LINE
Traditional

Allegro

❶   ❷   1   4

mf

4   1   4   4

D Str.   G Str.

112. Barcarolle from "The Tales of Hoffmann"
Jacques Offenbach (1819–1880)
French Composer

Andante   *To Coda* ⊕

p

mp   *mf*

D.C. al Coda   ⊕

f   *mp*

113. Theme from "Capriccio Italien"

Peter Ilyich Tchaikovsky (1840–1893)
Russian Composer

114. Greensleeves

English Folk Song

115. I Saw Three Ships

English Carol

116. I'se the B'y that Builds the Boat

Canadian Folk Song

Gigue

from *Orchestral Suite No. 3*
for String Orchestra

Johann Sebastian Bach (1685–1750)
German Composer
arr. Jeremy Woolstenhulme

Steps to Success:

❏ Count and play in compound meters of $\frac{9}{8}$ and $\frac{12}{8}$ time

❏ Play in compound meters with correct notes and bowings

Cantabile = to play lyrically, in a singing style

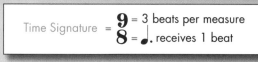

Time Signature = $\frac{9}{8}$ = 3 beats per measure / ♩. receives 1 beat

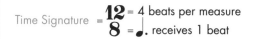

Time Signature = $\frac{12}{8}$ = 4 beats per measure / ♩. receives 1 beat

117. Three Groups of Three

118. Theme from Cello Concerto, Op. 85

Edward Elgar (1857–1934)
English Composer

Adagio

mf *cantabile*

119. Four Groups of Three

½ Pos.

120. Andante Cantabile from Symphony No. 5

Peter Ilyich Tchaikovsky (1840–1893)
Russian Composer

Andante

Steps to Success:

❑ Play in D Minor with 4th finger on F-Natural

❑ Understand half and whole steps in D Minor

4th finger on F-Natural

121. Finding D Minor in 3rd Position

122. Theme from Symphony No. 1

Gustav Mahler (1860–1911)
Austrian Composer

Adagio

mp

123. Spinning a Web

Andantino

mp – f D Str. D Str.

124. Rigaudon – *Duet*

Georg Philipp Telemann (1681–1767)
German Composer

Moderato

A

B

f

mf

Steps to Success:
❏ Use bow retrieval to accomplish good bow usage

125. A Change of Pattern   *TEST LINE*

126. Old Joe Clark   *American Folk Song*

127. Canon – Round   *Thomas Tallis (c.1505–1585)*
English Composer

128. Simple Gifts   *Joseph Brackett (1797–1882)*
American Composer

rit.

117SB

Steps to Success:

❏ Play notes D, E, F# on G string

❏ Play shifts by moving entire hand as unit

129. Shifting to 2nd Position

130. Sliding Into Second

131. Second Nature – *Duet*

132. Second Time Around – *Duet*

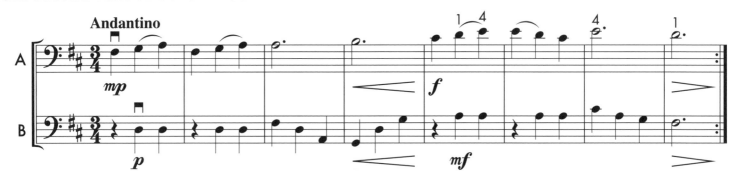

133. Playing Until the Last Second – *Duet*

134. Extended Hand Position

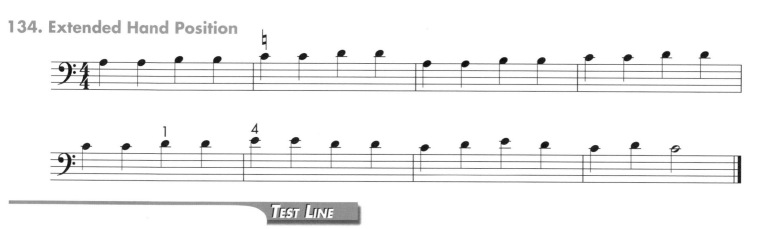

TEST LINE

135. First Finger Glider – *Duet*

136. Chico de Chile

137. Country Dance Party – *Duet*

Steps to Success:

- ❑ Understand E♭ Major key signature
- ❑ Play ½ position on the D string
- ❑ Play in E♭ Major in ½ position

A♭: *1ˢᵗ finger on G string*

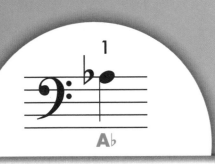

A♭

E♭ Major = 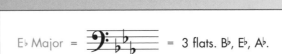 = 3 flats. B♭, E♭, A♭.

138. Adding A♭ – *Duet*

A

B

139. A♭ New Octave

140. E♭ Major Scale

141. Theme from Symphony No. 5

Ludwig van Beethoven (1770–1827)
German Composer

142. Ach, Du Lieber Augustin

German Folk Song

Steps to Success:

❏ Play in E♭ Major on G and D strings

❏ Understand half steps in E♭ Major

143. March in _____ Major

Fill in the blank above and mark the half steps.

144. Fresh Rain – *Duet* **TEST LINE**

145. Child's Play

146. Tingalayo

Caribbean Folk Song

117SB

Steps to Success:
- ❑ Understand E Major key signature
- ❑ Play in ½ position on the D string
- ❑ Play E Major scale

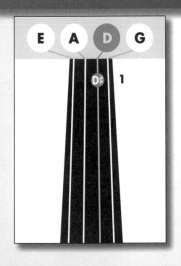

D#: ½ position on D string

E Major = 4 sharps. F#, C#, G#, D#.

147. Adding D♯ – *Duet*

148. E Major Scale

149. E Major Broken Thirds

150. Willkommen, lieber schöner Mai, D. 244 – *Round*

Franz Schubert (1797–1828)
Austrian Composer

Andantino

151. ½ Position is Great!

117SB

152. The Mulberry Bush **TEST LINE**

English Folk Song

153. Allegro from String Quartet No. 4, K. 157

Wolfgang Amadeus Mozart (1756–1791)
Austrian Composer

154. The Glendy Burke   Practice this line on an open string first to learn the rhythm.

Stephen Foster (1826–1864)
American Composer

155. The British Grenadiers

English Folk Song

156. Steps to Learning Theory

Add accidentals to play the melody in E Major.

Steps to Success:

❏ Identify differences between natural, melodic & harmonic minor scales in different keys

❏ Play natural, melodic & harmonic minor scales in different keys

Natural Minor Scale	= Half steps occur between the 2nd & 3rd and 5th & 6th notes of the scale. *See #157.*
Harmonic Minor Scale	= This is similar to a natural minor scale except that the 7th note is raised a half step. *See #158.*
Melodic Minor Scale	= When ascending, the 6th and 7th notes (of the natural minor scale) are raised a half step, and when descending, the notes are the same as the natural minor scale. *See #159.*

157. D Natural Minor Scale

158. D Harmonic Minor Scale

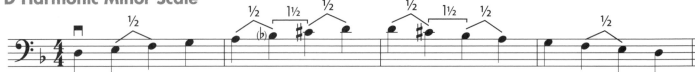

159. D Melodic Minor Scale

160. G _____ Minor Scale – *Steps to Learning Theory* 👣

Write the name of this minor scale on the line above.

161. E Melodic Minor Scale – *Steps to Learning Theory* 👣

Add the appropriate accidentals to make this a Melodic Minor scale.

162. C Melodic Minor Scale

163. C Harmonic Minor Scale – *Steps to Learning Theory* 👣

Write a one-octave scale reflecting the title. Use quarter notes as in 157.

164. Joshua Fought the Battle at Jericho
American Spiritual

165. March Slav – Orchestra Arrangement
Peter Ilyich Tchaikovsky (1840–1893)
Russian Composer

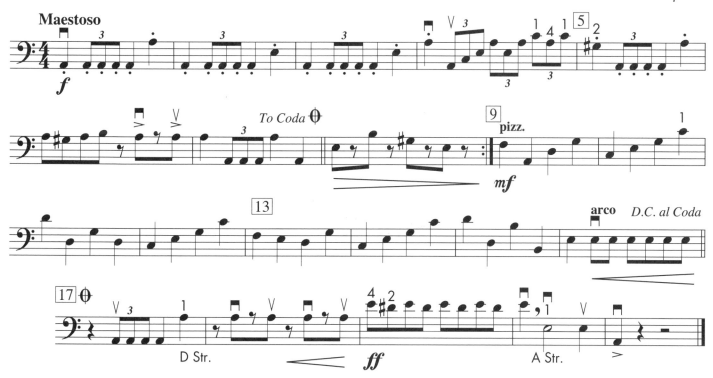

166. Chorale in E Minor – Orchestra Arrangement
Johann Sebastian Bach (1685–1750)
German Composer

Steps to Success:

❑ Understand grace note notation

❑ Play grace notes

❑ Play spiccato at a fast tempo

Grace Note = an ornamental note printed in small type

167. The Gypsy Baron Overture

Johann Strauss, Jr. (1825–1899)
Austrian Composer

168. Turkish March from "Six Variations for Piano, Op. 76"

Ludwig van Beethoven (1770–1827)
German Composer

169. Spiccato in B Minor

170. It's All About the Bowings

171. Can Can from "Orpheus in the Underworld" – *Duet*

Jacques Offenbach (1819–1880)
French Composer

172. Steps to Learning Theory

Name the major key for each key signature below.

Vibrato = a pulsating effect made by repeatedly rolling the pressed fingertip slightly forward and backward and is generated by the left hand/arm. Because the finger moves forward and backward so quickly, the pitch varies slightly to create vibrato. Vibrato produces an expressive and warm tone and adds intensity and depth to your playing.

Bassists will develop arm vibrato. It is done by rocking the arm, allowing the finger to be pulled back and forth on the string.

❏ The left hand, arm, and shoulder must be relaxed. Tension throughout your body will make vibrato nearly impossible to achieve.

❏ The thumb will be hovering slightly above the back of the neck. It must not squeeze down. The real pressure comes from pulling the arm back into the neck and not squeezing the thumb.

❏ Your thumb will move along with the finger slides.

Finger Slides F→E→F (♩ = 72)

These finger slides will look like you are polishing your string. Try these exercises without the bow first, then add the bow once you have correctly accomplished the slides.

REMINDER: Your thumb should be relaxed and flexible, and it should move along with the sliding motion.

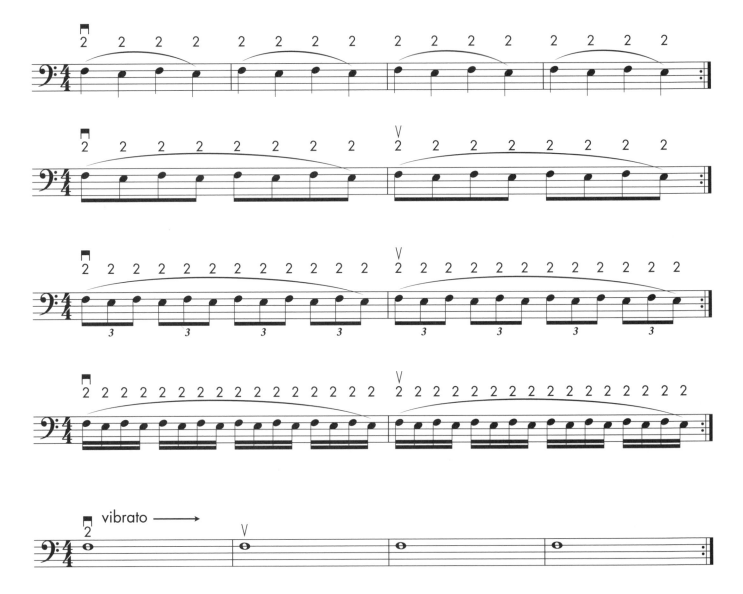

Finger Slides G→F♯→G (♩ = 72)

Finger Slides E→D♯→E (♩ = 72)

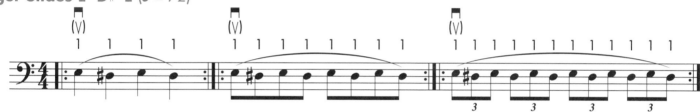

Finger Slides A→G♯→A (♩ = 72)

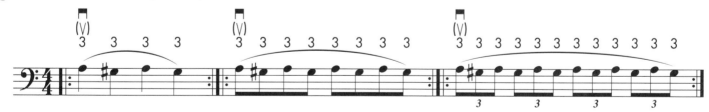

Glossary

a tempo *(7)*

Return to the original tempo after a **ritard.** or a fermata.

Adagio *(9)* [Italian]

One of the slowest tempo marks in music, slower than **Andante**.

Andantino *(14)* [Italian]

A tempo mark indicating a speed slightly faster than **Andante** and slower than **Moderato**.

Arpeggio *(13)* [Italian]

A series of notes which make up the 1st, 3rd, 5th, and 8th notes of the scale.

Bow Retrieval *(28)*

Technique used when needing to bring the bow back near the frog so that a short eighth note up bow (∨) stroke can be played.

Cantabile *(33)* [Italian]

To play lyrically, in a singing style.

Chromatic Scale *(17)*

A series of 12 ascending or descending half steps.

D.S. al Coda (Dal Segno al Coda) *(15)* [Italian]

Go back to the sign and play until reaching "To Coda," then jump to the Coda.

Eighth Note Triplet *(28)*

 = ♩ = 1 beat

Glissando *(24)* [Italian]

A continuous sliding of pitch from one note to another. It can be used as a special effect.

Grace Note *(44)*

An ornamental note printed in small type.

Harmonic (Natural) *(24)*

Special flute-like tones created by lightly touching the string at specific locations along the fingerboard. Harmonic notes are notated with a small o and a 3.

Key Signatures

A Major *(10)*

B♭ Major/g minor

C Major/a minor

D Major/b minor

E Major *(40)*

E♭ Major/c minor *(38/42)*

F Major/d minor

G Major/e minor

Louré *(9)* [French]

A style of bowing featuring long hooked legato notes. There is slight separation between the notes.

Minor Scales *(42)*

A series of eight notes in a particular stepwise ascending and descending order with a specific pattern of whole steps and half steps. There are three forms of the minor scale:

Harmonic Minor Scale

Half steps occur between the 2nd and 3rd, and 5th and 6th notes of the scale. The 7th note is raised a half step.

Melodic Minor Scale

When ascending, the 6th and 7th notes of the natural minor scale are raised a half step, and when descending, the notes are the same as the natural minor scale.

Natural Minor Scale

Half steps occur between the 2nd and 3rd, and 5th and 6th notes of the scale.

Modulation *(21)*

Changing from one key to another within a composition.

9/8 Time *(33)*

3 beats per measure and a dotted quarter note receives one beat. The conducting pattern for 9/8 time is:

Presto *(30)* [Italian]

A tempo mark indicating very fast, faster than **Allegro**.

Shifting *(18)*

A sliding or gliding motion with the left hand and arm to move from one position to another.

Simile or sim. *(14)* [Italian]

Continue playing in the same way such as with articulations and/or bowings.

6/8 Time (Fast: Counting in Two) *(30)*

2 beats per measure and a dotted quarter note receives one beat. The conducting pattern for fast 6/8 is:

6/8 Time (Slow: Counting in Six) *(29)*

6 beats per measure and an eighth note receives one beat. The conducting pattern for slow 6/8 is:

12/8 Time *(33)*

4 beats per measure and a dotted quarter note receives one beat. The conducting pattern for 12/8 is:

Vibrato *(46)*

A technique that produces an expressive and warm sound made by the pulsating effect generated by the left hand and arm.